CRAGGY THE COO

BY NICOL NICOLSON

*For my Mum, Kate Nicolson,
who created Craggy as well
as creating me. Thank you
for your unerringly positive
influence on both of our
journeys.*

CROWVUS
CHOUGHS

First Published in 2021
Crowvus, 53 Argyle Square, Wick, KW1 5AJ

ISBN: 978-1-913182-32-8

For comments and questions about
"Craggy the Coo"
contact the publisher at the_team@crowvus.com

www.crowvus.com

Sligachan, Isle of Skye

Rockcliffe, Dumfries and Galloway

I'm Craggy the Coo and I live a sad life.
I haven't a house or a job or a wife.
But I have a kind heart. I've got so much to give.
I just need some love and a fine place to live.

I'll search and I'll strive and I'll sing as I roam,
Until one day I find the right place to call home.

Edinburgh

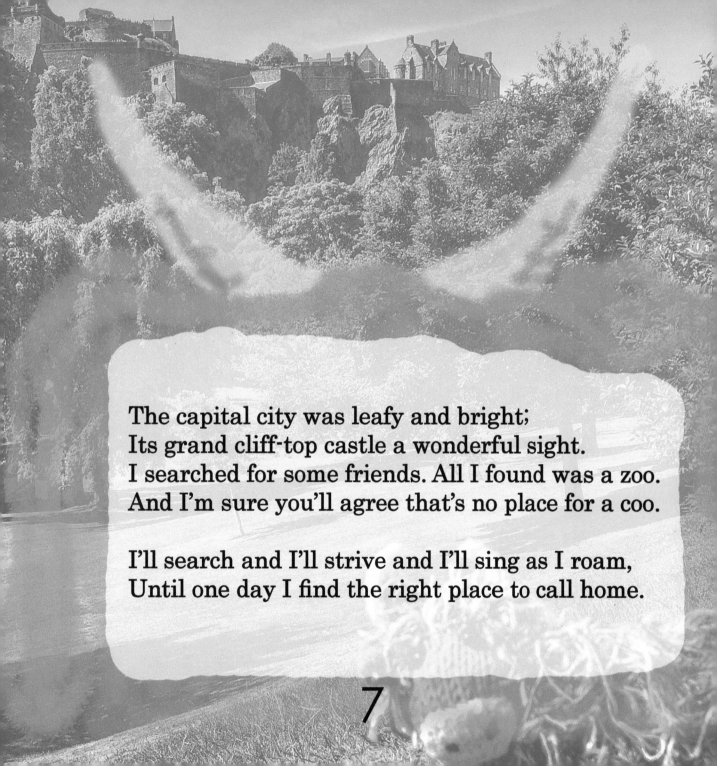

The capital city was leafy and bright;
Its grand cliff-top castle a wonderful sight.
I searched for some friends. All I found was a zoo.
And I'm sure you'll agree that's no place for a coo.

I'll search and I'll strive and I'll sing as I roam,
Until one day I find the right place to call home.

Glasgow

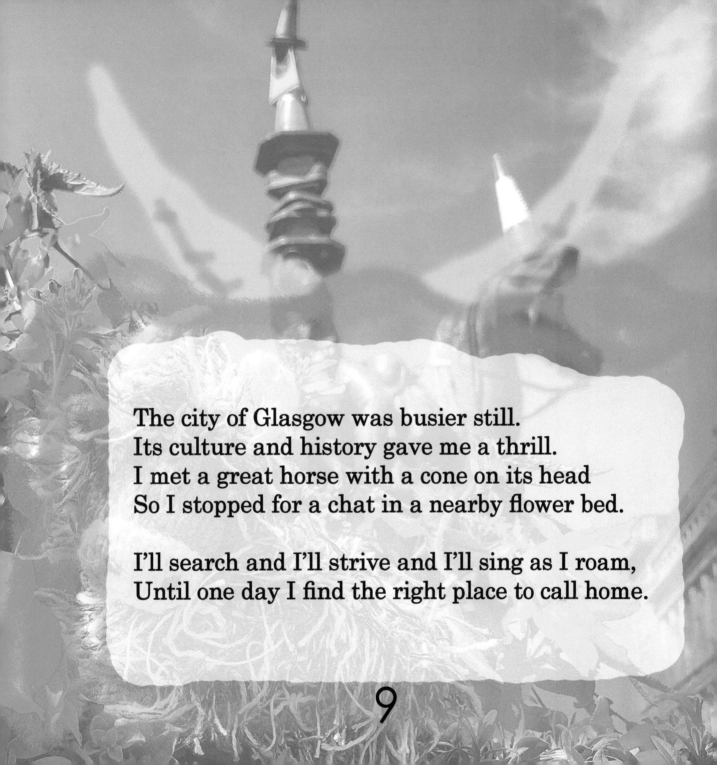

The city of Glasgow was busier still.
Its culture and history gave me a thrill.
I met a great horse with a cone on its head
So I stopped for a chat in a nearby flower bed.

I'll search and I'll strive and I'll sing as I roam,
Until one day I find the right place to call home.

Lunga, Treshnish Isles

In the west of the country I sat near the sea.
It was sunny and warm. I was calm as can be.
The puffins were friendly and let me come near.
But they fled for the winter and left me in fear.

I'll search and I'll strive and I'll sing as I roam,
Until one day I find the right place to call home.

Tobermory, Isle of Mull

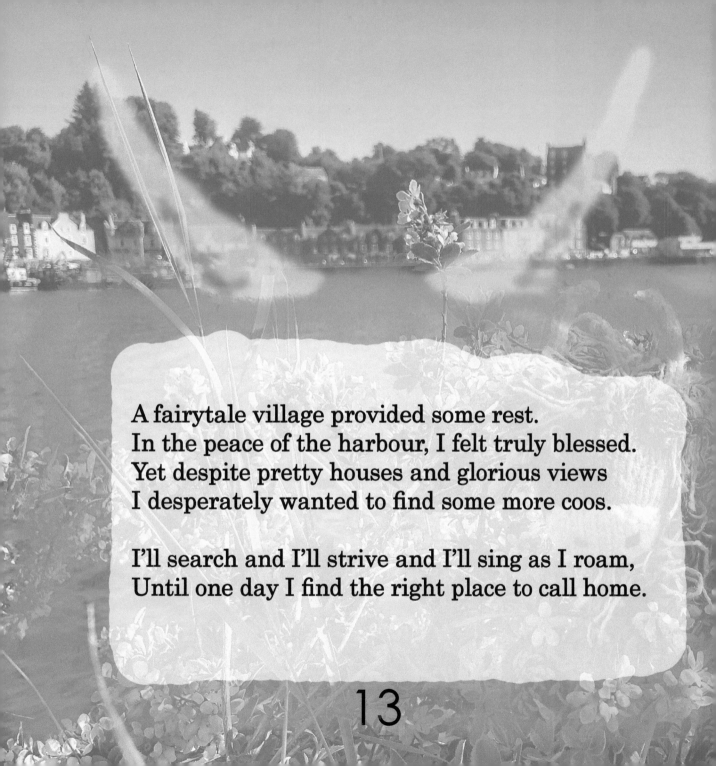

A fairytale village provided some rest.
In the peace of the harbour, I felt truly blessed.
Yet despite pretty houses and glorious views
I desperately wanted to find some more coos.

I'll search and I'll strive and I'll sing as I roam,
Until one day I find the right place to call home.

Suilven, Sutherland

I climbed a high mountain. It filled me with awe.
But with so many rocks, I had nowhere to gnaw.
The landscape around me was eerie and vast.
I began my descent before daylight had passed.

I'll search and I'll strive and I'll sing as I roam,
Until one day I find the right place to call home.

15

Bone Caves, Assynt

As I made my way down, I encountered a cave.
It was bleak. It was dark. I felt terribly brave.
A stone was my pillow. My face was so cold.
This obviously wasn't a place to grow old.

I'll search and I'll strive and I'll sing as I roam,
Until one day I find the right place to call home.

Forth Bridge, South Queensferry

I returned to the Lowlands 'til spring came around.
Despite a year hunting, no home had I found.
But my heart's in the Highlands. I vowed to go back
With a soul full of hope and my mission on track.

I'll search and I'll strive and I'll sing as I roam,
Until one day I find the right place to call home.

Loch Ness

I headed back north and stopped off at Loch Ness.
The wind was ferocious. My hair was a mess.
I saw no sign of Nessie and though the gale blew
I was sure I could make out a faraway "moo".

I'll search and I'll strive and I'll sing as I roam,
Until one day I find the right place to call home.

21

Home

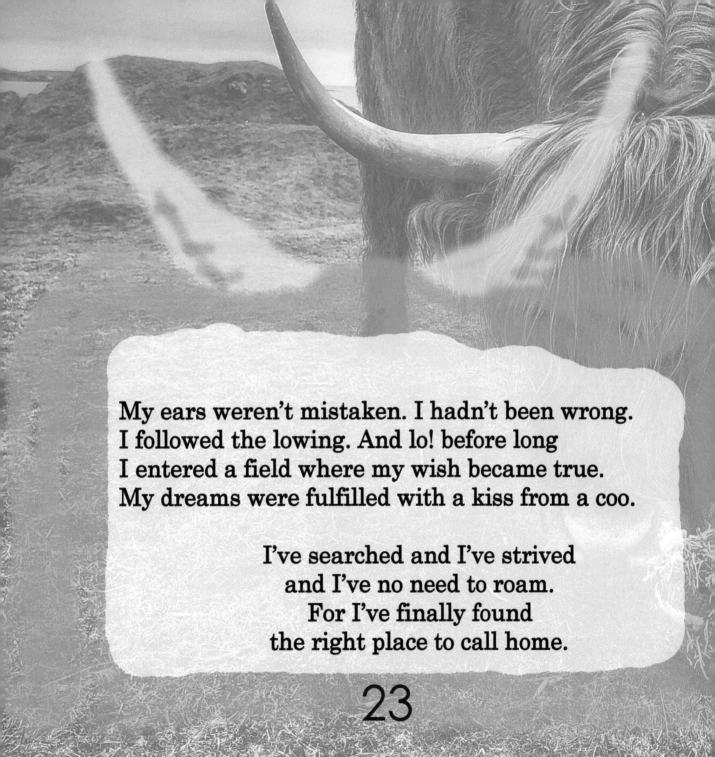

My ears weren't mistaken. I hadn't been wrong.
I followed the lowing. And lo! before long
I entered a field where my wish became true.
My dreams were fulfilled with a kiss from a coo.

I've searched and I've strived
and I've no need to roam.
For I've finally found
the right place to call home.

23

Black Cuillin, Isle of Skye

Lightning Source UK Ltd.
Milton Keynes UK
UKHW050646250421
382537UK00003B/81